CONTENTS

GREAT AMERICAN AUTHORS

Langston Hughes

by Jennifer Joline Anderson

Content Consultant
Christopher C. De Santis, Professor of African American
Literature, Illinois State University

CORE
LIBRARY

Published by ABDO Publishing Company, PO Box 398166, Minneapolis, MN 55439. Copyright © 2013 by Abdo Consulting Group, Inc. International copyrights reserved in all countries. No part of this book may be reproduced in any form without written permission from the publisher. The Core Library™ is a trademark and logo of ABDO Publishing Company.

Printed in the United States of America, North Mankato, Minnesota
112012
012013

♻ THIS BOOK CONTAINS AT LEAST 10% RECYCLED MATERIALS.

Editor: Kari Cornell
Series Designer: Becky Daum

Cataloging-in-Publication Data
Anderson, Jennifer Joline.
  Langston Hughes / Jennifer Joline Anderson.
    p. cm. -- (Great American authors)
  Includes bibliographical references and index.
  ISBN 978-1-61783-768-5
  1. Hughes, Langston, 1902-1967--Juvenile literature. 2. Poets, American--19th century--Biography--Juvenile literature. 3. African-American poets--19th century--Biography--Juvenile literature. I. Title.
  818/.5209--dc23
  [B]   2012946815

Photo Credits: Hulton Archive/Getty Images, cover, 1; Fred Stein Archive/Getty Images, 4; Library of Congress, 7, 23, 45; Apic/Getty Images, 10; AP Images, 12, 34; North Wind/North Wind Picture Archives, 15; Red Line Editorial, 19, 39; Universal History Archive/Getty Images, 20; Olga Matseyko/Shutterstock Images, 25; Bettmann/Corbis/AP Images, 26, 29, 31, 37; Bebeto Matthews/AP Images, 41

CHAPTER ONE

Becoming a Poet

Langston Hughes was on a train to Mexico in 1920 when he was 17 years old. It was a long trip from Cleveland, Ohio, to his father's ranch in the town of Toluca. Langston was feeling gloomy. His parents separated when Langston was small, and he had only seen his father a few times. They did not get along. Now he had just graduated from high

Langston Hughes sitting at his desk in 1954

school and would be spending the summer with his father. He was not sure how the trip would go.

When he was sad, Langston always poured his feelings into poetry. He got out his pen and an envelope he had in his pocket. The train was just crossing the Mississippi River, and Langston gazed down at the muddy waters below. He thought of his ancestors, the African-American people who had been sold into slavery. They had traveled down this same river to the plantations of the South. Then his mind wandered to other rivers in the world. He thought of the Congo in the heart of Africa and the Nile in Egypt. He thought of the Euphrates in Asia, where ancient civilizations had begun.

"I've known rivers," he wrote. "My soul has grown deep like the rivers." His hand moved quickly as he scribbled the lines on the back of the envelope. Fifteen minutes later, he had written a new poem, "The Negro Speaks of Rivers." Later that summer, he sent the poem to Jessie Fauset, a black editor and

Langston often turned to poetry to express his feelings. Many of his poems speak of his African-American pride.

writer in New York. She published the poem in *The Crisis*, an African-American magazine, when Langston was 19. It was the first time one of his poems appeared in a major publication. It was written in simple language yet had deep meaning.

Following a Dream

During that summer with his father, Langston wrote many poems. He felt out of place in his father's

African-American Magazines

In the early 1900s, new African-American magazines were created to help share black writing and ideas. One was *The Crisis,* founded in 1910 by W. E. B. Du Bois. *The Crisis* is the official magazine of the National Association for the Advancement of Colored People (NAACP), a group that still fights racism today. Another important magazine was *Opportunity: A Journal of Negro Life.* The editor, Charles Johnson, encouraged many young black writers. Langston Hughes had numerous poems published in *The Crisis* and *Opportunity.*

world. James Hughes was wealthy and successful. But he was also bitter and angry. He had moved to Mexico because laws in the United States made it impossible for him to practice law. Now he wanted Langston to leave America too. He wanted Langston to go to school in Switzerland and Germany, where he could learn to be an engineer. Then he could find a good job in Mexico working for a mining company.

Langston did not like this idea. Engineers needed to use a lot of math. Langston didn't want to study math, especially in a different language. He knew he wanted to be a writer, not an engineer. And he did not want to go to Switzerland or Germany. Instead, he had another place in mind: Harlem, New York.

To Langston Harlem was a dream city. It was a center of culture that attracted people of color from around the world. Many black musicians, actors, artists, and thinkers lived and worked in Harlem. He longed to see new black musicals on Broadway and hear the latest jazz and blues music in the nightclubs. He wanted to experience a city bustling with

Harlem, New York

Harlem is a neighborhood in Manhattan, which is part of New York City. In the early 1900s, large numbers of black people from the South moved to Harlem in search of a better life. Since then, the population of Central Harlem has been mostly African American. In the 1920s, Harlem was the center of an international black arts and culture movement known as the Harlem Renaissance. Langston Hughes was very involved in the movement. His stories and poems captured the spirit of Harlem.

Poet and playwright Langston Hughes in his 20s

people who were black like him. And he wanted to write about it all.

At last Langston's father agreed to send him to Columbia University in Harlem. Langston left for New York City in the fall of 1921. He never did study engineering. Instead he followed his own path.

"The Negro Speaks of Rivers"

I've known rivers:

I've known rivers ancient as the world and older than the

flow of human blood in human veins.

My soul has grown deep like the rivers.

I bathed in the Euphrates when dawns were young.

I built my hut near the Congo and it lulled me to sleep.

I looked upon the Nile and raised the pyramids above it.

I heard the singing of the Mississippi when Abe Lincoln

went down to New Orleans, and I've seen its muddy

bosom turn all golden in the sunset.

I've known rivers:

Ancient, dusky rivers.

My soul has grown deep like the rivers.

Source: Langston Hughes. "The Negro Speaks of Rivers," The Crisis,
June 1921. Print. 71.

What's the Big Idea?

Read this poem carefully. How do you think the poet is feeling? Is the voice he uses happy or sad? What is the poem's main idea?

CHAPTER TWO

Growing Up

James Langston Hughes was born in Joplin, Missouri, on February 1, 1902. He was named after his father, James Hughes, but his family called him Langston. His parents separated when he was a baby. He lived with his mother, Carrie Mercer Langston, but she struggled to support her only child. She moved to different cities to find jobs. She left Langston to be raised by his grandmother, Mary Leary

A young Langston Hughes in his boyhood hometown of Lawrence, Kansas, in 1914

Raid at Harpers Ferry

In October 1859 abolitionist John Brown and several others raided a military arms warehouse at Harpers Ferry, West Virginia. They planned to take all the weapons and start a rebellion against slavery. Their plan failed. All the men were either captured or killed, and John Brown was hanged. But the daring raid at Harpers Ferry lit a spark. Two years and many more clashes later, the Civil War began. By the end of the war, slavery was outlawed in the United States.

Langston, in Lawrence, Kansas.

Grandma Mary's Stories

Grandma Mary was a gentle, dignified woman. Langston loved her very much, but he was lonely without his parents or any siblings. They were poor and often had only salt pork and wild dandelion greens to eat. When Langston felt sad and alone, he escaped into the wonderful world of stories. His grandmother had many magazines and books in the house, and he read them all. But he especially loved to sit on his

Abolitionist John Brown holds one of his dying sons in the Battle of Harpers Ferry.

grandmother's lap while she told him about heroes from the past.

The stories she told were all true. Grandma Mary's first husband, Lewis Sheridan Leary, had died in the famous slave revolt at Harpers Ferry, West Virginia. His grandfather, Charles Langston, was an abolitionist who spoke out against slavery. His great-uncle, John Mercer Langston, had been the first black Congressman from the state of Virginia. Her stories made Langston proud to be an African American. Years later, he wrote a poem called "Aunt Sue's Stories," inspired by his Grandma Mary.

Langston's grandmother died when he was 12 years old. Remembering her stories made him brave. "Nobody ever cried in my grandmother's stories. They worked, or schemed, or fought. But no crying. When my grandmother died, I didn't cry, either," Langston later wrote in his autobiography.

Class Poet

After Grandma Mary died, Langston moved to Lincoln, Illinois, to live with his mother. Langston started eighth grade at a new school. He and one other girl were the only black students. He was popular and known as a good writer. Langston was elected class poet. At graduation he read a poem he had written about his teachers and classmates.

In 1916 the family moved to Cleveland, Ohio, and Langston went to Central High School. There he had friends who were black and white, Jewish and

Catholic. He published poems in the school magazine, *The Belfry Owl.*

Cleveland and the Great Migration

When Langston and his family lived in Cleveland, the city had a large population of African Americans. Most of them came from the South. They had moved north during the Great Migration to escape racism in the southern states. But racial discrimination was strong in the north as well. Black people were only welcome in certain neighborhoods. Landlords charged black families higher rent than what white people paid.

Early Influences

One of Langston's favorite poets was Paul Laurence Dunbar (1872-1906). The son of former slaves, Dunbar became the first African-American poet to become known around the world. His poems often used African-American dialect, or the language of everyday conversation. Hughes found Dunbar's poetry real and inspiring. As a high school student, Langston wrote: "My soul is full of color / Like de wings of a butterfly." He was writing in the style of Dunbar.

Langston's family could only afford small, cramped attic or basement apartments.

African Americans also had more trouble finding work. His stepfather worked long, grueling hours at a steel mill. It made Langston sad to see his stepfather wearing himself away so the family could eat. Langston wrote a poem, "Steel Mills," in which he described the mills "That grind out steel / And grind away the lives / Of men."

Journey to Mexico

When Langston was 17 he spent the summer in Mexico with his father. He was not happy there. His father was rich. He owned a vast ranch and many apartment buildings in the city, but he treated his employees poorly. He even forced Langston to sit for hours adding up figures. "Seventeen and you can't add yet!" he would yell when the numbers did not add up right.

By the end of the summer Langston never wanted to see his father again. But after he graduated from

The Great Migration, 1910–1930		
City	**African-American Population**	
	1910	**1930**
Chicago, IL	44,103	134,000
Cleveland, OH	8,500	72,000
Detroit, MI	5,741	120,066
New York, NY	91,709	328,000
Philadelphia, PA	84,500	220,600
St. Louis, MO	45,000	94,000

The Great Migration

From 1910 to 1930, between 1.5 and 2 million blacks moved north to escape racism in the South. In just a few decades, large northern cities, including Cleveland and New York's Harlem neighborhood, became centers of African-American life. The Great Migration changed American culture in many ways. Look at the chart above. What does it tell you about the Great Migration?

high school, he returned to Mexico. He hoped to convince his father to send him to college. Langston showed his father his poem "The Negro Speaks of Rivers." It was printed in a magazine, *The Crisis*. Finally James Hughes gave in. If his son could get a poem published at such a young age, perhaps he could become a success after all.

CHAPTER THREE

Across the Ocean

Hughes enrolled at Columbia University in September of 1921, but he felt out of place in the mostly white school. After one year Hughes dropped out, and his father stopped sending him money. He looked for a job, but time and again he was told, "I didn't advertise for a colored boy." Finally, in June 1923, he was hired to work on a trade ship bound for Africa.

As a young man, Langston Hughes was drawn to the social scene in Harlem.

As the ship headed across the ocean, Hughes felt relieved and excited. He was 21 years old now, a grown man. And he was ready to learn from life.

African Shores

Hughes's ship stopped at ports in Senegal and Nigeria, on the western coast of Africa. Even here Africans were ruled by white people from Europe. The white people treated Africans unfairly, just as whites in America treated blacks unfairly. This made Hughes angry. He told the Africans he understood their problems because he was black too. To his shock, they didn't believe him—they thought he was a white man.

Like many African Americans, Hughes had a mixed racial background. His skin was coppery-

Inspired by Africa

Hughes was one of the first American poets to use African themes, or ideas, in his work. In Africa, he often heard the beat of African drums. One of his poems, "Danse Africaine," describes a dancer moving to the beat: "The low beating of the tom-toms . . . / Stirs your blood. / Dance!"

Langston Hughes poses for this photo by Gordon Parks in 1943.

brown, not black, and his hair was wavy, not curly. But he still felt a strong connection to the African people. He wrote many poems about his experiences on African shores and sent them home to Harlem. A whole page of Hughes's poems appeared in the August 1923 issue of *The Crisis*.

Springtime in Paris

In the spring of 1924 Hughes traveled to Paris with only seven dollars in his pocket. He struggled to find a job and a place to live. Fortunately, he found work in a nightclub. As he washed pots and pans in the kitchen, he heard the sounds of jazz and blues. African-American music was in style throughout Europe. Hughes included this beat and flavor in his poetry. One of his poems, "Negro Dancers," captured the rhythm of two people dancing to jazz. Hughes sent his poems home to New York, where they were published in three magazines.

Love in Paris

While in Paris Hughes fell in love with a girl named Anne. Her father was African and her mother was English. They talked of marriage, but Hughes felt he was too poor to support a wife and family. Anne's father also did not approve of the match, so the two parted ways. Hughes never married. He wrote a sad poem about his lost love called "The Breath of a Rose." In 1928, the poem was made into a song by the composer William Grant Still.

Paris felt like home to Langston. He loved hearing the rhythms of the African-American jazz and blues that were popular in the nightclubs there at the time.

FURTHER EVIDENCE

There is quite a bit of information about Hughes's travels in Chapter Three. How did his travels influence his writing? Read about Langston Hughes and find some of his poems on a Web site, or look in his autobiography *The Big Sea* to find more information about his travels around the world. Find a quote to support the idea that Hughes's travels inspired his writing. Does the quote you found add a new idea to the chapter?

Langston Hughes's Poetry
www.english.illinois.edu/maps/poets/g_l/hughes/hughes.htm

CHAPTER FOUR

Renaissance in Harlem

When Hughes returned from Europe he found his reputation as a poet had grown while he was away. Many people had read his poems in New York magazines, and they were anxious to meet him. But being a promising young poet did not bring a regular paycheck. Hughes lived with his mother and brother in Washington DC. He found work at a wet wash laundry. Later he worked

African Americans dance at a Harlem nightclub in the 1930s. Nightclubs were gathering spots for poets, artists, and musicians during the Harlem Renaissance.

as a busboy in a hotel restaurant, setting and clearing tables. The jobs were not glamorous or literary, but Hughes enjoyed spending time with ordinary working people. He wrote poems about the people he met. One of these poems, "A Song to a Negro Wash-Woman," was published in *The Crisis* in January 1925.

Hughes and the Renaissance

In the spring of 1925 Hughes received an award of $40 for a poem called "The Weary Blues." Later he included it in a brand-new book of poems, also called *The Weary Blues*. It was published in January 1926 by Knopf when

Busboy Poet

In December of 1925, the well-known poet Vachel Lindsay held a poetry reading at the hotel where Hughes worked. Hughes wanted to meet Lindsay and hear his poems. But black people were not allowed in the auditorium. So he copied three of his poems and set them beside Lindsay's dinner plate. The next day, Hughes learned Lindsay had read the poems to his audience. Newspapers carried the story that Vachel Lindsay had discovered a "busboy poet."

This famous photograph of the "busboy poet" was snapped by a press photographer after Langston's poetry was praised by well-known poet Vachel Lindsay.

Jazz and Blues

Jazz and blues are musical styles with African roots. Both were developed by African-American musicians between the late 1800s and the early 1900s. Blues came from African-American spirituals, or religious songs, as well as from work songs and chants sung by slaves as they worked. Jazz combines African rhythms with European musical styles. Hughes loved jazz and blues, and he often invited musicians to play along with him as he read his poetry.

Hughes was 24 years old. Critics loved the book.

In 1926 Hughes enrolled at Lincoln University, a black college in Pennsylvania. Every summer he went back to Harlem. This was the period known as the Harlem Renaissance. During the 1920s, the African-American art, literature, music, dance, and theater happening in Harlem became known around the world. For the first time African-American artists were being recognized. At the time blacks were often stereotyped as humble servants, clownlike characters, or evil thugs. But the black

African Americans dance the famous Jitterbug in a
Harlem nightclub in the 1930s.

EXPLORE ONLINE

Langston Hughes was a key figure in the Harlem Renaissance. Read over the information on the Harlem Renaissance at the end of Chapter Four. Then visit the Web sites below to learn more. Compare and contrast the information in this book with the information you find online. What can you learn about Langston Hughes and the Harlem Renaissance from the Web sites?

The Harlem Renaissance
www.pbskids.org/bigapplehistory/arts/topic9.html
www.brainpop.com/socialstudies/ushistory/harlemrenaissance

people who appeared in the art and literature of the Harlem Renaissance were real and complex. Hughes's writing was at the center of the exciting new movement. His poetry spoke truthfully about the African-American experience—both the good and the bad. It had the rhythms of blues and jazz. And it was written in a simple, honest style that most people could understand and appreciate. It was no wonder Langston Hughes became known throughout the world as the voice of Harlem. He expressed the hopes and dreams of African-American people.

Excerpt from "My People"

Dream-singers,
Story-tellers,
Dancers,
Loud laughers in the hands of Fate—
*   My people.*
Dish-washers,
Elevator-boys,
Ladies' maids,
Crap-shooters,
Cooks,
Waiters,
Jazzers,
Nurses of babies,
Loaders of ships,
Porters,
Hairdressers,
Comedians in vaudeville
And band-men in circuses—
Dream-singers all,
Story-tellers all.
. . .

Source: Langston Hughes. "My People," The Crisis, June 1922. Print. 72.

Nice View

Hughes wanted African Americans to be recognized as equal to whites. What is he saying about African Americans in this poem? Compare this poem with "The Negro Speaks of Rivers" on page 11. How are they similar or different?

CHAPTER FIVE

Spreading the Message

After Hughes graduated from college in 1929, the Great Depression hit. Thousands of Americans were out of work, and nobody had money to spare for a book of poetry. So Hughes traveled around the country reading his poems. He charged whatever his hosts could afford—sometimes $50 or $25—and sometimes nothing at all.

This photo was taken in 1961, when Langston Hughes was active in the Civil Rights Movement.

Jim Crow Laws

Beginning in 1876 many states in the South passed laws that segregated blacks from whites. These laws were named Jim Crow laws. The laws stated that blacks could not attend school or eat in restaurants with whites. On public buses, they had to ride in the back. Some states passed laws that made it hard for blacks to vote. Black people who broke the laws were sometimes beaten or even killed.

In the South, Jim Crow laws made it difficult for Hughes to travel. Hotels and restaurants had signs saying, "No Negroes Allowed!" But he was welcomed in black colleges, clubs, and private homes.

Hearing Hughes speak opened the eyes of young African Americans. Some of his poems, such as "My People," praised the beauty of African Americans and encouraged black pride. Other poems used strong language to protest racism. This made southern whites angry. Hughes was banned from speaking in some places, and guards were hired to make sure violence didn't break out.

When Langston Hughes traveled during his poetry tour in the 1930s, he saw signs like this all over the southern United States.

Hughes ended his poetry tour in San Francisco, California. He had traveled across the country reading his poetry. In doing so, he spread an important message about racial equality.

More than a Poet

Hughes also wrote novels, short stories, a two-volume autobiography, and nonfiction books to teach young people about African-American heroes. He wrote operas, musicals, plays, and he even created his own theater company in Harlem in 1938. It was

Hughes on Broadway

Beginning in 1942, Hughes wrote a weekly column for a black newspaper called the *Chicago Defender*. The column featured a comical character named Jesse B. Semple, or "Simple." Through Simple, Hughes used humor to talk about serious racial issues. The character Simple became so popular that Hughes published five books and wrote a Broadway play based on his stories.

called the Harlem Suitcase Theater because all the equipment they had could fit into one suitcase.

Poetry and the Civil Rights Movement

Slavery had been outlawed in 1863, but the dream of racial equality kept getting put off. People grew tired of waiting. In the 1950s and 1960s, African-American anger fueled the Civil Rights Movement. During this time of social unrest, masses of people fought for African-American rights. Hughes expressed his anger in his poetry. He protested racism and called for America to fulfill the dream of equality for all citizens, white and black.

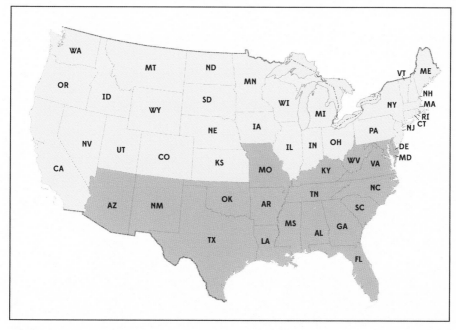

Jim Crow South

This map shows all the states that had Jim Crow laws in red. The laws were different from state to state. They separated blacks from whites in education, public transportation, hotels, restaurants, hospitals, prisons, and other areas of life. During the Civil Rights Movement, large groups of black people protested these racist laws.

Hughes dedicated his last book of poems, *The Panther and the Lash,* to Rosa Parks, a hero of the Civil Rights Movement.

A Writer's Legacy

Sadly, Hughes did not live to see the end of the Civil Rights Movement. He died suddenly after complications from surgery on May 22, 1967. Hughes's death was mourned all over the world. But his funeral was like a celebration. Jazz and blues music were played, and people read his poems aloud. His life's work had touched many people. Although people were sad when he died, they were grateful for the gifts he left behind.

During his lifetime, Hughes's writings spread the message of equality. His poems showed that black people were beautiful and had much to be proud of. They taught people of all races how to love themselves and each other. His success broke new ground for black writers everywhere. Today nearly 100 years after the Harlem Renaissance began, Hughes's works are still read and enjoyed. His influence remains strong and his legacy lives on.

The Langston Hughes House in Harlem, New York, is where the famous poet lived until his death in 1967. The house is now a historic landmark.

IMPORTANT DATES

1902
Hughes is born in Joplin, Missouri, on February 1.

1916
Moves with family to Cleveland, Ohio.

1920
Graduates from high school. Moves to Mexico to live with his father for the summer.

1921
His first national publication of a poem, "The Negro Speaks of Rivers," appears in *The Crisis* magazine. Moves to New York City to attend Columbia University.

1925
Discovered by poet Vachel Lindsay in December while working as a busboy in Washington DC.

1926
Enrolls at Lincoln University in January. His first book of poetry, *The Weary Blues,* is published.

1967
Dies in New York City on May 22 at the age of 65.

KEY WORKS

The Big Sea and *I Wonder As I Wander*

Hughes's two autobiographies. *The Big Sea* covers his early life and experiences during the Harlem Renaissance. *I Wonder As I Wander* covers the decades that follow.

Hughes, Langston. *The Big Sea*. New York: Knopf, 1940.

Hughes, Langston. *I Wonder As I Wander*. New York: Rinehart, 1956.

Five Plays

This collection of Hughes's plays includes *Mulatto*, his first Broadway play, and *Simply Heavenly*, a musical comedy based on the Simple character from Hughes's newspaper column.

Hughes, Langston. *Five Plays*. Ed. and Introd. Webster Smalley. Bloomington, IN: Indiana UP, 1963.

Montage of a Dream Deferred

This book contains a series of poems written in a jazz style. They show short scenes of life in Harlem and call out the need for social change and justice for African Americans.

Hughes, Langston. *Montage of a Dream Deferred*. New York: Holt, 1951.

Not Without Laughter

This novel tells about an African-American boy named Sandy. Hughes based the book partly on his own memories of growing up in Lawrence, Kansas.

Hughes, Langston. *Not Without Laughter*. New York: Knopf, 1930.

The Weary Blues

Hughes's first poetry collection, this book contains some of his most famous works, including the title poem "The Weary Blues," "The Negro Speaks of Rivers," and "Aunt Sue's Stories."

Hughes, Langston. *The Weary Blues*. New York: Knopf, 1926.

Take a Stand

This book discusses how Hughes tried to use his poems to spread a message about racism. Do you think poetry can really make a difference in the world? Write a short essay detailing your opinion, reasons for your opinion, and facts and details that support those reasons.

Dig Deeper

What questions do you still have about Langston Hughes? Do you want to learn more about his life or read some of his poems, stories, and plays for yourself? Write down one or two questions to help guide you in your research. With an adult's help, find reliable new sources about Langston's life and work that can help answer your questions. Write a few sentences about how you did your research and what you learned from it.

You Are There

Imagine that you visited Harlem during the 1920s, at the height of the Harlem Renaissance. Write 300 words describing your stay. What bands or musical acts did you see? Which authors and artists did you meet?

Tell the Tale

This book discusses Langston Hughes's life. Write 200 words that summarize the true story of how he became a writer. Be sure to set the scene, develop a sequence of events, and write a conclusion.

GLOSSARY

abolitionist
a person fighting to abolish, or end, slavery

autobiography
a story of a person's life, written by that person

civil rights
rights held by a citizen of a free nation

discrimination
unfair treatment of a group of people based on race, gender, age, religion, or some other characteristic

Great Migration
the mass movement of southern African Americans to the North to escape racism during the early 20th century

heritage
something that is passed down or inherited

legacy
something passed down from one generation to the next

novel
a long work of fiction

protest
to stand up against an idea or law

racism
unfair treatment of people based on their race

segregated
separated by race

stereotype
an overly simple opinion about a person or group

LEARN MORE

Books

Hughes, Langston. *Langston Hughes.* Ed. David Roessel and Arnold Rampersad. Illus. Benny Andrews. New York: Sterling Publishing, 2006.

Hughes, Langston. *The Big Sea: An Autobiography.* 1940. New York: Hill and Wang, 1993.

Walker, Alice. *Langston Hughes: American Poet.* Illus. Catherine Deeter. New York: HarperCollins, 1974, 2002.

Web Links

To learn more about Langston Hughes, visit ABDO Publishing Company online at **www.abdopublishing.com.** Web sites about Langston Hughes are featured on our Book Links page. These links are routinely monitored and updated to provide the most current information available.
Visit **www.mycorelibrary.com** for free additional tools for teachers and students.

INDEX

ABOUT THE AUTHOR

Jennifer Joline Anderson has been writing since she was a teenager. She lives with her husband and children, Alex, Ruby, and Henry, in Minneapolis, Minnesota, where she writes educational books for young people.